Possible Lives

Possible Lives

Poems by

Jon Ballard

Cover design by Shay Culligan

ISBN: 978-1-952326-79-0

Kelsay Books
502 South 1040 East, A-119
American Fork, Utah, 84003

For my daughters—I love you more

"You're so American. You believe everything is possible, everything will come…"
—James Salter, *Light Years*

Acknowledgments

Grateful acknowledgment is made to the publications in which the following poems first appeared:

Blue Earth Review: "Restoration," "The Math"
Blue Monday Review: "To China"
Boxcar Poetry Review: "Railroad Crossing," "The Man Who Comes to Visit"
Breakwater Review: "Daybreak"
Broadsided: "Late"
Cimarron Review: "Fresh Air, 1971"
Connecticut River Review: "Winter Burial"
Finishing Line Press (Chapbook): "Turning In," "Demolition Man"
Flint Hills Review: "How It Was Or Wasn't," "The Messenger"
Foothills Publishing (Chapbook): "Complicity"
Grey Sparrow Journal: "Grandmother At 91"
Innisfree Poetry Journal: "Snowbound Traveler"
Maverick Duck Press (Chapbook): "The World"
The MacGuffin: "Foraging"
Midwest Review: "A Life of Their Own"
New Mexico Poetry Review: "Model," "Each Longing Unlike the Rest"
New Plains Review: "Housewife"
Oklahoma Review: "An Afternoon, Say," "Previous Life"
Pudding House (Chapbook): "Never Once," "Cousins"
Quay: "West of Homer, Michigan"
Schuylkill Valley Review: "Little Ones"
Third Wednesday: "North Country Thaw," "Bad Movie"
Valparaiso Poetry Review: "The Peach Orchard"
Weave: "Lending An Ear"

Contents

III—How It Was or Wasn't

I—A Life of Their Own

Model

The mouth parts demurely, yes, and the hips
move—as the box promises—*like the real thing.*
But the eyes blame me already for multitudes:

the broken promise of perfection, all
the leftover pieces sitting on the table
I couldn't figure out how to work in.

A dancer's step. A saint's resolve. The artist's passion.
The clockmaker's care. All tricky feats
of workmanship, requiring the small-

motor skills of tradesmen or minor gods—
out of my league. She can't be consoled, though—
my mistake of fitting in *the heart's desire*

and *a soul's stirring.* She sits on the floor,
naked and flushed as a newborn, looking
away now toward the open window,

the birdsong. More than I ever intended.

Field Work

When humans forget
a field the field
rejoices, seeds itself
with buzzing and distances
and wind miscellanea.
Here the trees brood
kindly over root
rights-of-way
and sunlit views,
and which grove or
other is responsible
for attracting the wrong
kinds of birds.
Pasture the County
doesn't care to cut
grows to the height
of a man's knee,
though such a measure—
the grass blades agree—
is a shoddy gauge
of wildness.

The Messenger

He says writing a poem isn't
so different than treading out
onto a frozen pond, those first
hesitant footfalls on the glazed
surface, coupled with the back-
of-the-mind dread that the winter
weight you put on might be enough
to send you crashing through,
added to the knowledge that you
cannot swim, compounded by
the reality that you are all alone
in this foolhardiness and no one
waits within shouting distance
to pull you out or run for help.
Okay, okay, he concedes, in truth
writing a poem is not as fraught
with danger as all that. It doesn't
kill or maim the corporeal vessel,
and no insurance company yet
has found it profitable to offer
coverage against improper usage,
the soul-dismembering failures
of intention, or the hot-blooded
metaphors of the heart. But it's not
picking daisies, either, he wants
to make clear. Or maybe it is
at that. He seems weary, then,
the kind of tired that makes you
glad he isn't cutting out a spleen,
or operating heavy machinery.
He starts to mutter something about
the ritual fumbling for right words,
the lazy midnight ransacking
of earlier moods, about kissing

the comely girl who kisses you back,
the girl who braves uncertainty,
who sticks by you years to see
how it will all turn out. By then
you wonder aloud if he's still
talking about writing a poem, or
if he's moved on slyly to another
subject—his love life, say—
words he seems to apprehend
in that crestfallen mode
of blundering messengers
everywhere. A look that admits
he's managed to find the wrong
house, to knock on the wrong
door. How it turns out he's been
wasting your precious time. How
all along he's had you mistaken
for someone else.

To China

Reminded this is your father's shovel, used once
for crushing a prowler's skull. Another time to scoop
fresh pug dung onto the neighbor's lawn. The old man
had what they called *nerve*, though the blotter downtown
said otherwise: *rabble-rouser, disturber-of-the-peace, lout.*

Midnight is no time for digging: surveilling neighbors
tug each other's robe sleeves behind damask curtains.
Stars leap your head like loot-bearing thieves over
ornamental fences. Your wife flits past the door-wall,
wearing nothing. Nothing you haven't seen before.

Your dog-eared copy of *Colloquial Mandarin*
and a sack lunch ready to go. Goodbye letters stacked
between the two made-in-China gnomes
the local ironists will claim started it all.

A Life of Their Own

We had names picked out
for the children we didn't want.
Not unlike the cooking school
in Tuscany you'd never open,
or the novel of ideas I'd fail
to draft mornings on the portico
overlooking our make-believe
vineyard, lying that way was
some hokum we'd settled on
early. *William* and *Lorelei,*
you dreamed once, and so they
became. The boy's hair grew fair,
longish, while his bones carried
on your line's fey delicacy, so
that our fear for him—fresh meat
for the savages—receded only
when his voice broke one day
like a pickaxe into ice. As for
the girl, from the start she knew
her place in the world: barnstormer
among all the earth-leashed
muddlers—she might soar if we
just stepped off her wings. Of
course we were anxious, not
easy to convince. We'd had
friends whose real daughter ran
off over nothing more than
a boy's raffish smirk (even now
they must cast a wary eye
on roadside ditches as they pass).

O, Lorelei, faux child, unwanted
but secret favorite of our many
pretenses, you scared us
most of all. We live each day
relieved, or should I say grateful,
that you were never born.

Town Hall Lore

And then of course the crackpot in the bunch
chimed in, his madness silencing the crowd
like a gavel's righteous rap, or a child's scream.

Some ladies pulled their purses closer, while
the lone door guard scratched his ear with one
hand and slipped the other over his baton.

People that night remembered hearing the old crazy's
diatribe on the slippery slope of generals pressing stick-
pins into maps—how it always leads to catastrophe

and woe. Others swore they heard a great lecture
on metaphysics, buried somewhere between laments
on the ubiquity of plastic grocery bags stuck

in trees, a paucity of naked nymphs in the modern
world, the infinite mixed signals of all our gods.

Your Little Wonders

Say you'd written a thousand
poems, each one with
a fine pair of tawny legs or
a set of golden wings, heading
out into the world with
names like *Josephine* or
Muriel, but each
meeting on its way
hard-edged, hairy-backed
prose—*Carls* and *Sams*—
that liked nothing more
than explicit backseat romps,
sometimes peeing in the neighbor's
daises after an evening of
drinking or snorting or downing.
There's nothing you could do
to save them—they'd be
in the world, a party to it,
yet naïve and hamstrung
by a certain small beauty
that says *devour me* or
ignore me, for which you'd
blame yourself all night long
and for many years,
while your muse worked
in the backroom nonstop
with your blessing
at breaking your own heart.

Restoration

This morning you are like Chekhov
at Yalta, coughing up a lung, a wooden
bowl of apples on the table beside you.
Summer porch, air that should cleanse,
the indelicacy of sickness, the short breaths
of so many intimations—all you can do
is watch the lady with the toy dog go by
though you've known her and she
has loved you—or it was another woman
like her, her love the blushing kind,
fretful, summer dresses and bare feet,
eating all your little apples to the core while
you slept, while you slept and devoured her.

Nightshift

His late-hours job involved cataloguing
and indexing the infinite sorrows,
then filing reports to the man upstairs.
His approach was scholarly, in that
it precluded any paw at the soul.
The woman who strove to love him
wondered if he might not be willing
to try a new line of work, like appraising joy
or charting the occurrence of miracles.
Say a day job with a work-life balance,
in an office park in the suburbs, maybe
his very own reserved parking space?
"But what about job security?" he argued,
watching her eyes grow as dark and moisty
as plum pits, her quaking lips, her arms folding
like false armor against him. (It would all
be in his report later on, especially the eyes.)

History Lessons

On the day H decided you were an arsonist
playing with matches, the whole forest burned.

Once or twice a woman sought your indulgence,
only for H to hint in her vaguely exotic tongue

that you should let her down. No accident, then,
you've waked alone in many rooms that H chose

and furnished in her own spartan taste—every wall bare,
every table and chair faux-distressed. Sometimes

H saw to it that your dog died in the street, or
that a call you made to a parent seeking forgiveness

never made it through. H barely tolerated you,
truth be told. So that many a winter evening when you

started to write the story of your life, H intervened.
Suddenly the one working bulb in the room might

flicker and die. Then the pilot light in the old furnace
would refuse to catch. Meanwhile, your reliably staid

neighbors would go shrill with late-night humping.
The Montblanc in your hand, just like that, going dry.

Metaphysician in Repose

Abyss-night: neither hammer nor
lullaby, but somewhere in the cosmic-
middle's droning dominion.
You stare for hours afterward at the living
room wall where one of Rivera's
flower vendors has kneeled for years,
unduly fraught with blossoms.
So many times you've wanted to offer
a hand, but chose instead to wait
and see what happened next. Waited
for that sombrero to lift and show
you it's really Juarez or Pancho Villa
hiding under there. Maybe even
Frida in drag, or Trotsky betting
that a basket of lilies and a floppy hat
will save him yet from assassins.
Chosen as you have this night
one of several possible states
of being, anything could happen.
Not bloody likely, the kettle shrieks
from the other room. But still.

An Afternoon, Say

On the periphery of some vast imponderable.
Sitting there with you in an open-air café,
sipping the crummy house brew. I comment
on our rube of a waiter—on the wait staff
in general, aproned harbingers of the apocalypse—
until you marshal a defense: *People do what they can.*
Meanwhile, your name and accent have all
but escaped me, even as your beauty, I fear,
cloaks a nihilist's bent (though nothing pleasantly
surprises like being dead-on about a stranger).
Now a breeze topples a flower vase the next
table over, water sopping the white linen
like the spilled blood of a thousand cockroaches.
The stable of waiters passes a single cigarette,
laughing in unison, pall on our afternoon.
Say my name, you whisper, accompanied by
a kiss, a surreptitious grope under the linen.
Whatever-your-name-is, listen: it's useless.

Complicity

Old man in the park refusing
to feed the pigeons, listening
instead to passers-by disparage
the morning for its sunless sky,
its unexpected chill, all the banal
distresses of a malfunctioning day.
Winter-lean squirrels, sloven as dish-
rags, mulling about, while dark birds
chase down the dawdling trees
in wing-tipped pairs. Leaves of
innermost boughs no one ever hears
edgy now in the sough of wind.
A woman on her cell phone saying,
"—my lunch—I brown-bagged it—
it's gone and no one knows anything."
That's right, thinks the old man,
so near to weeping for the world,
burping instead, licking his lips.

Scene of the Crime

In most such reveries nothing ever
really happens—seldom "relations,"
as your genteel conscience puts it;
"a nuzzle here and there," submits
the overtaxed, under-paid public defender
that is your inner voice, and always
in that same dubious, plea-deal-ready timbre.
Waking these fretful dawns beside
your wife, you've half a heedless mind
to rouse her, apologize for throwing over,
in dreams at least, this true-blue life
you've forged, and all for a pretty-
and-willing-thinged-elsewhere
every paunchy man of middle age
knows to be a lie. In the end you leave
her be, the half of your mind that knows
never to wake a spooning giant
weighing in at last, preserving order
like a patrolman at the scene
of the crime, chasing off gawkers
with little more than an indomitable
glare, a wordless warning that says
keep it moving, nothing to see here.

Previous Life

Think of it now in terms your memory
won't robotically abhor: moonlit walks, say,
but this time each of us strangers on opposite sides
of the street. Your kisses like pawned jewels
bought back in solvent times. Letters to me
now all scribbled in *Anon's* feverish hand.
Your books with my dog-ears smoothed out,
or failing that, lost in a grease fire or night theft
you failed to report. All of it is easy
to imagine; erasure or revisionist history—
call it what you want. Whatever empowers
you or makes you roar (however the women's
magazines codify it these days). Because now
that I'm gone I'm here to help; I want for you
nothing but the best. Please pretend I mean it
when I say such things, the way you always did.

Late

What you love about the calendar is its tidy
largess of days, asking neither that you live
well nor do good with the gift it's made.

But because everything has a beginning,
a middle, and an end, and you are, reasonably
speaking, somewhere in the late stages

of the middle, you await the beginning
of the end as if a human solstice, the inexorable
waxing or waning: the fading of natural

blondness or a rise in unprovoked pissyness,
or a sudden flushing at the mere mention
of sex, a primness after your grandmother's,

who by this age had loved (unofficially)
so many fewer men than you. Yet years
of looming ebb haunt you less than this

very night, which is coming on fast, chasing
you down like you were the thief of some-
one's last loaf—sourdough or rye, let's say.

Cousins

You haven't spoken to Solitude in years,
though sometimes he levitates above you
anyway in the scatter-shot oak leaves
during afternoon walks, or accompanies
you to the toilet at dreary dinner parties.
In the mirror he comes off looking
like your twin, slightly balding,
the farmer's tan, the eyes that dart
down or away like a swallow glancing
hillsides. But it's Solitude's second cousin
Loneliness who sticks her foot in the door
every chance she gets, and she's got
a beautiful arch, a podiatrist's dream.
When you're done sucking her toes
each night she kicks in your teeth
and says, "Back tomorrow for more," while
Solitude watches from your window ledge,
feeding crackers to the pigeons, not a voyeur
(though he likes the toe action) so much
as an anxious observer, a friend
who doesn't know what to say.

Lending an Ear

God vanished down a rabbit hole,
says the old man, in between bites
of stiff bread crust (you wonder
that his teeth don't come out).

His seat in the diner is reserved—
Like my stool in hell, he quips.
He's an ex-preacher from down
Arkansas way, or an insurance man—

he can never quite decide. Claims a son
returned after years in the wilderness,
only to pinch a Jackson from his wallet
then disappear later the same day.

Try a Danish, he pitches, fiddling with
his wristwatch. *It stopped eleven years
ago…the repairman said it would
be cheaper to just go buy a new one.*

Before the evening is through he'll
explain how trees have as many souls
as leaves *(So what does that make
a lumberjack, I ask you?);* that he used

to box a little, until he killed a man; that
the man he killed had taken the Lord's
name in vain—*Not that he deserved to die,
mind you, but don't we all of us have it coming?*

The Man Who Comes to Visit

1.

Three butterflies flying together
will bring good luck, though if any of their wings
touch, the moon will fall on your lover's house.

2.

Three seagulls flying together means imminent death,
though if any of their feet touch waves, your lover
will be out of the house when the moon crashes in.

3.

Dropping a fork means a man will come to visit.
When the man comes he will say he's your father
and offer you cut rate lessons in stoicism and logic.

4.

Dreaming of acorns foretells pleasant things. But the man
who visits when you drop your fork will tell you to spurn
your dreams like he did his love, and not to bother with the moon.

II—A Picture Book of Michigan

Railroad Crossing

The train a lament on wheels:
the word *cruel* graffitied
onto one hopper car, *kaput*
on another—annotations
on the planet's sorry state
or just artists' dour handles.
My daughter in the backseat
observing, wondering where
all the passengers are.
"It's not that kind of train,"
I say, watching her lips
after my explanation
fashion the word *boxcar*
with the same scary awe
the Pentecostal daycare
has taught her to say
Jehovah. We've just come
from there—agnostic
fan of cheap daycare
and God-fearing child.
But now here we sit,
ten minutes and counting
at the railroad crossing.
Flat cars, tank cars, gondolas—
slow procession of metal
with supplementary notes
from the underground:
duel, heed, rash, qualm.
Then a stenciled Jesus or
maybe Che Guevara minus
the beret. Either way
the face of an interloper,
no caboose in sight.

West of Homer, Michigan

Perhaps the meaning of the world
out there among the tidal fields,
though you're only passing through.

Rows of corn—the kind of symmetry
God shunned. (Was it Jesus in His
workshop, parking sawhorses side
by side, who made us love such tidiness?)

Red sky at morning. The side of a barn
never that red still telling a black-
lettered, years-ago message: *It's a boy.*

Out of the darkened barn,
a farmer carrying a red pail, shiny
boots in the exquisite dew.

North Country Thaw

Between queuing pines, hallway
of rain. Haggard drifts sheer white

on the forest bed, ephemeral still,
pocked with melt. March its own

beautiful enemy, turn-coat, snake-oil
peddler, conjurer of imprudent buds.

Nearby, the muddy two-track a proverbial
road to nowhere, ruts of the earth,

dark passage, settlements of rain
and run-off, dung of the world.

A Picture Book of Michigan

*The city of Flint, Mich., is in the midst of a water crisis
several years in the making.*

—Washington Post

Midcentury curio—
printed before riots
or rust or kitchen
taps spewing lead
at twenty-seven
parts-per-billion—
it opens with a bit
from Longfellow's
Hiawatha—
"By the shores of
the Gitche Gumee…"
Checked out last
from Cloverdale
School library, May
of '68, by a child
rummaging
history or trivia
or pretty pictures,
unaware how
in those days
they hand-stitched
innocence
straight into leather
spines, and darker
truths hid
like Minnehaha
in her wigwam
dying of famine
and fever.

Photographed Outside the Pine Dale Motel
Grand Bend, Ontario, Canada, 1960

Hand on his slim, thin-belted hip,
grin of a thousand provisional charms
he'd no doubt already deployed
with great success on the credulous,
the unwary, the born-every-minute
girls of the sort the world never
seems in short supply—*that* man
went on to father four boys
with two women, to divorce
and remarry, then divorce again.
To scapegoat the whole wide world
with each inevitable slipup.
To sit alone in darkened rooms,
as if like Count Dracula himself
he'd finally reckoned, after years
of caustic forays into the lights
of earth, that night or its facsimile
was the only tolerable condition.

Grandmother at 91

These are the days when nothing
is made possible by desire alone. Bedrailed,
diapered, cathetered, grace's exile,
the age of bones, of skin as amorphous
as some bleak geography from 20,000 feet.
By the bathroom scale scribbles on a pad
of paper: her daily recorded weights
(102, 102, 100, 97, 99, 94, 92...), the proof
we like to have in numbers of what goes on
right before our eyes. Caretaker daughter,
a son who drinks and inquires after
the life insurance; grandsons who do
nothing more than stand by, relieved
of duty by miles or estrangement
or the high hurdles of the diffident heart.
She gapes as the visiting nurse Theresa
rattles on about her cats, her car problems,
the need for her patient to get out of bed.
Theresa's bejeweled hands appraise her,
molecularly gentle (dare I say a *saint's* touch?).
Grandmother says "Huh?" to a question
no one asks, deaf even to the silence now.
To my unspoken pleas for Theresa to shut
up about the cats, to take her junker
on down the road to the next invalid.
Goddamned gypsy nurse—words on the tarmac
of my tongue, waiting to take flight.
Of course I keep silent, as does Grandmother:
pluck-less, devoured by hungry years, frowning
a little at all the fuss. All the dragging
on of things, all the dragging out.

Housewife

That kitchen devoured
Mother, sopped her up
in butter and bacon fat.
Stool-high cupboards
that stuck, never bare
but empty a way
only she could see.

One window over
the counter grimed
by greasy eons—pried
open for lilacs two
weeks in spring
every year, the only
perfume she wore.

Hers and No One Else's

Wind as blue collar
as that town, hauling
whatever was given it,
union in its regular
demonstrations. There,
Mother bit clothespins,
Protestant by default,
wordless hour upon hour.
Syllables she didn't form
got choked back—hers
to swallow, by god,
and no one else's.

Father: A Possible Origin Story

As if an emissary
in ill-fitting shoes
sent by the Empire
of Unhappy Men (a land
no doubt as big and thirsty
as Russia, minus
the poetry).

Alleyway

Rain-ruts graded and smoothed, gilded
with new oils, fresh road to the kingdom.
Hoofed in file, footprints behind us
in the turned dirt, stampede's aftermath.
The gang's stragglers percussive, all trashcan
lids and whittled sticks. Nothing then
but scruffy sovereignty. Streetlights burning
dim fanfare. Returned from august lands,
met by masters nursing salty dogs, lit
and laughing in their wrought iron
patio chairs. Irked by intrusion,
indifferent to our claims of great, golden
caches, issuing last orders: *get to bed.*

Tending the Grave

Skies August and stringent.
Flat stone rose-hued and fiery
to the touch. Hotfooted ant
tracing chiseled grooves
marking death's date—
circuitous path barely
two years forged. Your
flower, pansies, planted,
watered to excess against
the day's heat, against
the months between now
and any foreseeable return.

You should see the latest
great-granddaughter feats—
acrobat still, but not quite
circus in her bones.
What Else? You've got
fresh company, one Mildred
Catherine Tilden, Chicago-born,
her flower geranium, garnish
of dusty miller. And sorry
to report: that young alder's
shade will need a few
seasons more to reach you.
Confession: how endurable
your absence is, though
grief's raw, bravura wound
once pledged otherwise.

Enough "gab" as you
used to say. So comforting
to know your hearing's better
now in that deep-buried
ash pot than it was those
last years among the living.
No longer any need to shout
just to catch you up, to speak
of ordinary things in a voice
better suited to bridging
chasms or punctuating
violence. A loudness, recall,
that brought the nurse
running from her station
the last time I saw you,
ready to find a madman
on the loose, keen perhaps
to discover something
in death's dull anteroom
beyond the obvious.

Little Ones

Puny dungareed fire-gods, we burned
worlds. Where we lived mothers didn't know
what they didn't know. Mornings our fathers
cleared lungs as if being born all over again.

We heard of wars out there we didn't play,
and how not dying in them was a rule
you couldn't make. Sticks we whittled into
unsheathed swords never put an eye out
no matter what parents prophesied. We
endured the way little ones do: cowering
when prudent, running when we had the jump.

Penny candies pillaged from Dunsky's
we traded in the park, our order
neither feudal nor basic-gang but
anarchic in their absence. Sometimes
fists told us what we'd get, settled things.
Cuts, bruises, pocketsful of Jujubes
parents might question or berate
or never notice if we played it right.

Fresh Air, 1971

Monster's heinous stride, thunder tracked us then.
Nerve, appetite, we braved raucous blocks, brown-
bagged salami and cheese heavy as rucksacks.
Slickers and black buckle-boots the lot. Rain
we tasted foundry in. Later, lunch scraps lured
crows our rocks scarcely hit. Windows could still
open: boys stuck their heads through to spit
whenever teachers stepped out of rooms. Hours
that school loved us. We pledged. Map of Michigan
our mitten, we pointed where we came from.
No money trees, adults chided, but the foundry
lasted fifty years and kept lunch pails in white
bread, pickled baloney, spam if men could bear it.
Good grades would get us in, or else a foreman
someone's father's uncle knew. Recess, we
watched those stacks spew what we'd tongue later
walking home. Our mothers barked weekends
to go outside and *get* fresh air: we hung on
clotheslines, hiked without permission to the old
asylum. Glad to gasp some danger. Lungful.

Demolition Man

Wanting you or anyone to tell me *stop,*
I scratch this rash of broodings. Later,
lamplight: fulsome blazes of nearby living
rooms slopping into the night like drunkards
cut loose at closing. This house can take
its shabby history with it. My window
looked slantwise on the world and still does.
Once, your unsentimental eye saw this lot
as hardscrabble and rut, but our own
and nobody else's. Remind me again
of all the worse-off out there. Grim mantra.
You had your theories though nobody cared
to know. And God never heard you except
as back-fence talk. Had such dwelling shut Him
out? Or something else within, less mortar
than melancholy? Any faith we ever forged
was bulldozed long before today, and besides,
my orders to obliterate are clear.

Nothing Prepares You

Perhaps you'll marvel
having awakened ten thousand
feet above the city, peering
slantwise into history's locus,
flinted lambency of eons, such
Roman patina. Easy in that moment
to knock American light, its
relative newness and naiveté,
insisting its waves and particles
rate exception—God's very own.
Easy to malign the New World
altogether. Back of you ocean
and half a sea, distance that gives
a traveler pause: too far
or not far enough? And later—
midday, say—eddying into and through
the Piazza di Spagna, reeling heat
and the first heal blister. A daughter
near, in pale relief, beguiled
enough to have quit all devices
and diversions. To have, without
coaxing or visible chagrin, taken
your hand in hers.

The Peach Orchard

An absence of bees, which
surprises—just us among
the laden, bejeweled trees.
One girl in the car sleeping,
the other trailing after you
like a handmaiden, picking
where you pick, gathering
what you gather. The basket
fills with more fruit than we
can ever eat. "I'll bring cobbler
to the office," you say,
tempering our cheery greed.
Already we've devoured more
than our share of happiness,
though the inequitable
universe seems aloof, unaware
of our years of good fortune.
Driving home the scent of
peaches laps through the car
as if we are in the company
of tides. The radio, meanwhile,
mentions darkening skies.
But not here, and not anywhere
we can see, not for miles and miles.

III—How It Was or Wasn't

Each Longing Unlike the Rest

The woman in line ahead of me, for instance.
Her grocery cart heaped with convenience,
inner ankles butterfly-branded, maybe more
in all those places you'd expect to net them.

Her hair the color of tropical sand—almost
no color. Waist thin enough to grope with slack,
to position with the feral ease of daydreaming.
But also the cold shower of a child at her side,

pushing a miniature cart with a small flagpole
announcing a *shopper in training.* The buggy's cargo
like a ransacked cliché: diapers, sanitized wipes,
two boxes of Honey Nut Cheerios. The girl

half-tapping scuffed Mary Janes, both pale arms
covered from wrist to shoulder in wash-away
butterflies, scorpions and spiders. Which brings
me back to Mama: her likely penchant for

arachnids, all that hidden ink like illustrations
of desire, a dark carnival of needs. Intimations
of the young woman *before,* childless, the modesty
her parents adored ready for carving up.

What Was Missing

She traveled by bus, spent
the night in the city for the first time
in years. The old hotel looked down
on new construction—a fast-food
joint with a drive-up window,
convenient for late-night bingeing.
A magazine ad had praised
the hotel: "Priced right, and close
to everything you want to see."
But she didn't want anything
the city had to offer after all.
She might as easily have gone
to the sea, which the room's
apropos-of-nothing nautical-themed
wallpaper—skiffs with spritsails
and schooners and ocean steamers
suspended in off-white space—
hinted was magical. At night under
lamplight she used the hotel's courtesy
pen to fill in what was missing.
Not just waves, but gulls and islands
and on the west wall below the faux-
jeweled mirror, the setting sun
like a pinprick on the horizon.
When she ran out of ink she sat
on the floor, back against the door
of her desert island. The palms
in the distance swooned like weary
ballerinas; the trade winds smelled of
burgers and fries. Down the hallway
footsteps, faint knocking,
the listless knocking of coconuts
thumping about in the trees above.

Daybreak

I

What bleak beauty to this place, like tramps chewing
onions open-mouthed in a field of rye. Already you see
the timber train high on the track where ticketless clouds
jostle and board. Stars out here some nights. Some nights
just the locals lit. Your yeses much too many for all
the naysayers about. Some common sham in the air inhaled
as covetously as second-hand cannabis, and what of it?

II

They say the undertow here accounts for much loss, while
the pastor patches up the rest like any good corner man.
No one ever taught you how to swim or even how to be
a man, thus you paddle like a mutt and live like a fool.
In the kiosk on Main Street the magazine covers
announce twenty ways to make her tingle; a dozen ways
to keep her guessing; nine ways to say you're sorry.

III

Such backwater. Houses still dark with thuggish love. Stars
smart to leave, while daybreak heralds the threadbare faiths,
their old and pleasing hymns, the creaking pews God
never winces at. Your own raw hands pocketed, fumbling lose
change and bits of lint. The offertory bowl rising and falling
on a tide of pious palms, half empty, coming your way.

Reaching

We watch gulls lunge,
all ravening appetite, swipe
pretzels from a couple's
hands outstretched over
a fourth-floor balcony.
The seabirds screech
with winged privilege,
the worst sort of pilferers:
indolent yet insistent.
The couple's scattershot
hooting self-reverential,
as if they've just invented
such lakeside idiocy.
We curse the racket,
birds' and humans' both—
all the cheeky wildlife—
plot and dodge feathers'
descent, loosed as if
from God's own pillow.
"Dirty birds," you judge,
then one last, longish pour
of the local cherry vino.
"Some people," I chirp,
aware then we've been
taking up sides without
saying so, as others
among the hundred balconies
must also have done.
"Could be a fable," you
posit, tipsy, playing up
the seagulls' crucial
presence, their scene-
stealing burlesque.
"More like a parable,"

I say, emphasizing
the couple, the basic
human factor at work.
Both of us aware neither
has it quite right, our
schooling in such matters
addled by wine, by years
of stray scenes defying
illumination, our reaching
for heftier meaning,
or failing that, any
minor consolation.

Bad Movie

Persuaded to imagine a different ending,
you and I exit through the popcorn
laden aisles, then out into the feral,

pouncing light of day. Lousy matinee
left us ill-intentioned, maybe: we
don't look away passing an accident

on the highway, obedient only to our
blood impulse, vulgar together instead
of the less pleasing solo kind. Later,

neither of us cringes when the late
local news brings us *Death on the Interstate.*
We listen as one survivor says it was

like being in a bad movie—cliché-bound
rube even in celebrity. He smiles,
farcically jubilant, while the moon contributes

its bright breadth to the limelight.
As for the dead: lone adult, cindered,
identification pending. Already we're

imagining the roadside memorial, its white
cross plunked down in the median against
the vacillating tide of goldenrod, yellow

flowers rippling as if in a movie's final frame,
and us, sitting in the dark afterward,
dissatisfied we don't know why.

Never Once

The woman of the house is washing
radishes from the backyard garden.
Her apron—a gift from grandsons
a thousand miles east—festooned
with a bushel-basket of apples, which
she fancies spilling out onto the floor
if she's not careful. When the phone
rings she rushes to answer, a habit
left over from busier years. A stranger
yelps, "It's never too late to refinance—"
She hangs up, against all the mores of
her upbringing. It's awful what people
make you do, she thinks, pawing
radishes on the counter like a makeshift
rosery, distracted then by the wisp
of children's voices, the neighbor boys
who sometimes come over and pretend
to eat the apples on her apron, smacking
their lips, rubbing their bellies like little
princes at a feast, never once asking
for the real thing (which she has),
preferring pretense, caprice,
the staggering flavor of make-believe.

Winter Burial

Dig here. Previous bones might be the thanks,
or rocks too stuck to budge. Gale-smacked,
windbreak poplars bent back like catapult arms.
Granddad holds weather talk is waste. His gin
mouth says you don't get to pick the day you die.

To him the pet cemetery means one more field
made profitless. He'd tidied pasture, shoved boulders
for Depression pennies. His hands learned to love
the heft of stones and women too. Coy he wasn't,
stories went: always lifting other boys' girls without
asking, showing how muscle was its own permission.

He loves cats as far as he can throw them, but
digs deep: Grandma knows his soul sings fields
though she'll always get her way. She sees snow
not as snow but poultice on this upturned earth.
To headwinds she purrs unchurch hymns, while
Granddad sinks the box he's cut to fit the beast.

How It Was or Wasn't

Women like crushed petals in your leather-bound history.
Midday light like the dresses they wore
then shed when dusk and your hands came down.
*

Once, a woman whose eyes even in repose exacted a toll.
And long letters, lusty imitations of love, drives
in the country, moon-blanched and heat-revved petting.
Leaves overhead suggestive of infinite un-joined hands
though applause was clearly in order.
*

And every once in a while discrepancies or fallacies
in your recollections, bewilderments
where you seemed to say and believe
selfless things, *do* them, and were beloved.

The Math

Accurate to account that our
bodies' joining was pure treachery.
That on five occasions—three
in parked cars, twice in motels
seedy enough to lockout love
while slipping desire the key—
we were faithless. Accurate to say
we knew our hearts were in it less
than our hyper flesh, and no matter
what, afterwards, we would be
diminished not because of sin,
but because we trusted wholly
in its absence. An accountant
of *rollicking-fun* might have debited
exactly twelve-hundred forty-seven
kisses, while the numbers-man
for *tangled web* could pencil in
no less than sixty-seven credits
between us of the cutthroat denials
of fault. Desire's double-ledger
could always show us the math
of our schemes, though of course
we never asked, certain we couldn't
be fooled into believing the numbers
added up to anything compared
to the truth as we'd come to know it.

Incurable

Bedlam in the winter trees, the snappish
lash of branches, starlings brusque
fly-by-nights under these whips of bark.

Climbing the parapet of wee hours
your bones know their age, creak in idioms
this youngish doctor can't quite make out,

his instruments and implements unlikely
to heal anyway, but torturous—cold and bluish
as your father's stingy, tobacco touch.

Later, you tell the cabbie to *slow, slow,* then *hurry*
through the dusky city, his Old-World eyes
sympathetic to the rift in your desires.

It Comes Down to This

Wise student of the world,
careful not to expect too much.
The theatrical darkness of windows nearby.
Within, let's say: mouth-breathers
of suburbia, the compass-less,
the rationers of desire and builders
of unholy contraptions. The none-
too-bright and the not-so-pleasant.

Love out there somewhere, says
the lady with the crystal ball, so be
patient; your time will come.
Your father once told you patience
was a sucker's bet. He who never
screwed up anything later
that he could screw up straight away.

So you don't need advice, or
prognostications. Though you've paid
this woman twenty bucks, and it's late,
and the lie that you'll have your chance
gets prettier every time you hear it.

Snowbound Traveler

His russet face and frame have something to say,
to teach you—a stranger—about the fields
in these parts; about shoveling the world: spring
snow—but also post-holes, fire-pits, manure-piles,
graves. His wife must be in some other part
of the old farmhouse feeding the cats
(if they don't have cats, you swear
you'll turn in your cynic's badge for good.)
Outside, March wind abuses porch chimes
into a vexing clatter; snow is driven high
against the grain silo, against your car—
podgy blue carcass—at the end of the drive.
Then the farmer's voice: "Sleep here
on the davenport. Morning the plow'll come."
He brings you pillows, blankets—no sign
of the wife—though the bedding, thin
and faded by years spent drying on
clothes lines in the sun, is covered in
cat hairs, red tabby you think, the wild
orange of Garfield the Cat, of this twilight.

Turning In

Hounded a little bit by the dusk
coming on just now like a pack
of dogs roaming the neighborhood
looking for light to snip at.
Our new, raven-haired neighbor
working the laundry-line, dark shawl
covering her shoulders the way my
arms would be at this very moment
if, for instance, I had ever knocked
on her door and charmed my way
in, played a few bars of Schubert or
Brahms on the piano I imagine sits
in her living room, at which I invent
my own musical brilliance in accord
with all the other necessary enchantments
to make a proper conquest of it.
"Her name is Maura or Maureen; she's
a divorcee from Tupelo or Tempe,"
my wife offers from our bed, to which
my return is all but certain, even now.

Under His Green Thumb

This latest fool-for-love
sent running semi-nude
to the curb, her bruises already
visible—clear as the fault
in his (now) munificent eyes.
Afterward, police like ants
on the untidy scene, the way
they converge then disperse,
the world plainly unchanged.

From his backyard garden
in the like-it-never-happened
aftermath, he sneaks a scurrilous
wink at me—uneasy neighbor,
911 caller—while his flowers
litter the plot with their
trifling majesties: dahlia
rakish in the evening's bleak
heat, black-eyed Susans
mustering like his long pageant
of mistresses tamed
into believing anything.

Late Local News

Night as off as this weatherman's act.
I watch his finger's indolent trail
along the coastal plain—a beachcomber
at heart? He offers next day's boaters
wave-height warnings, then something
about *E. coli* and all the beaches
closed or closing. Banter follows with
the anchorman over the general lack
of rain, the need to conserve water,
to be a good citizen. "I'd like to take
a long shower without feeling
like a criminal," the anchor kids, segueing,
smirk intact, to local reports of crime
and pestilence. My wife mouths a word—
insufferable?—at that very moment,
beautifully peeved (still not speaking
to me), all high and mighty in her
reading chair, thumb tongue-licked,
magisterial, turning pages loud
enough to papercut the air and me
both—slight, invisible wounds
meant to forecast this bedroom's
own enduring drought.

The World

As if I had critiqued aloud
the wild maneuverings
or hygiene habits of our taxi
driver, though I'd only observed
how the city was lit against
the night like a child's room
against bedtime monsters.

The corners of your mouth dim
in retort: how, for instance,
the world was a miracle even
then, huddled together in that taxi,
shuttled toward some get-together
for which you needed new
shoes and I—according to you—
a new silk tie, a trim, a new attitude.

Outside, the dark treetops blurring
past, flecks of light that might
have been stars, or else stones
in a far meadow echoing what
the moon had just said about
the world being overrated, all
the cities, all the little parties.

What You Wouldn't Do

She picks at her black-painted
nails, gives you her patented
it's-all-your-fault glare.
"Wherever we are," she snits,
"it's the wrong place."
And you begin to wonder
if she will ever be tender again.
Not *now* or *today* (you know
you don't rate such miracles),
but later on, maybe when
necessity dictates, that
bargain-basement leftover
you're none too proud to hoard.
But for the time being
the holding pattern is insolence,
the fixed pout of orphans
and midnight desk-clerks
(both of which she is)
who never stop longing
for strangers' grander lives:
that old chestnut of zero-
sum, how others' alleged luck
has come at her expense.
Hopeful, you're compelled
to imagine how, a year
from now, maternal, feeding
the cats milk and Cheerios
on her hands and knees,
her soul will alight on
a sweeter plane—honeybee
on petal, hummingbird
on filament. Her voice
will lilt like a river
valley breeze (though

the trailer-park will sit
in a dusty, treeless cove).
She'll glance up from
the floor—still spoon-
feeding cereal to the cats—
thinking out loud:
"Let's get a collie," or
"Buy me that ring we saw."
And you will.

Foraging

The doting way the spruce
and fern nudge in,
the old cabin seems birthed
of wilderness. Sandy earth
along the path bares
the roots of everything.
Here, furry mammals
saunter about, snouts
and whiskers twitching
and compassing,
like anxious men
foraging for praise.

Far from here, cubicles
maze their grey way into our
animal souls, and not
a single window opens.
The thermostat is locked at 67°
and the man with the key
has never heard the sound of rain
in the trees. Water cooler talk
shies past potluck Thursday
to last night's lotto,
which it seems no one won,
though everyone played.

About the Author

Jon Ballard's poetry and fiction have appeared in over sixty journals since 2006, including *Cimarron Review, New Plains Review, Flint Hills Review, Midwest Review, The Valparaiso Poetry Review, New Mexico Poetry Review, San Pedro River Review, Blue Earth Review, The MacGuffin, Boxcar Poetry Review, Connecticut River Review,* and *Broadsided.* He is the author of five poetry chapbooks, as well as a novel, *Year of the Poets (*Loose Leaves Publishing, 2014), which Kirkus Reviews called a "highly readable, character-driven debut." Jon currently lives with his family in southeast Michigan, where he works as an adjunct English instructor at Oakland Community College.

About the Author

www.ingramcontent.com/pod-product-compliance
Lightning Source LLC
Chambersburg PA
CBHW070335090426
42733CB00012B/2488